# Bullseye on Bullying

*Your Blueprint to Beating the Bullies*

BRYAN LEE

Global Touch Press
Happy Valley, Oregon

Copyright © 2021 Bryan Lee. All rights reserved.

No portion of this book may be reproduced mechanically, electronically or by any other means, including photocopying, without written permission of the publisher. It is illegal to copy this book, post it to a website, or distribute it by any other means without the permission from the publisher.

Global Touch Press
Happy Valley, Oregon

ISBN:
Printed in the United States of America

# Contents

Preface ................................................................. iv
Introduction ........................................................... vi
How to Use This Book ........................................... ix
Why Is this Book Written by a Clown? ...................... x
Did You Know? ....................................................... xi
What Is Bullying? .................................................... 1
Why Are Bullies Targeting Me? ................................ 6
Power vs. Authority ............................................... 11
Fact or Myth: If I Tell Someone, the Bullying Will Stop ....... 14
The 3 Bs of a Bullying Situation ............................. 18
Don't Be a Bully for Your Cause ............................. 21
Elder Abuse: Are Your Parents Safe? ..................... 23
How to Counterattack a Bully ................................ 28
How to Keep Bullies from Targeting You: Your Body Speaks .... 33
Workplace Bullying ................................................ 36
Is Publicly Shaming a Bully Bullying? .................... 38
Letter from a Bully ................................................. 41
You Are Better Than You Think You Are! .............. 46
How Clowning Cured My Bullied and Broken Soul .... 49
Get a Bully-Proof Blueprint ................................... 53
About the Author .................................................. 54

# Preface

NEVER LET OTHERS INTIMIDATE AND bully you ever again. This pocket manual gives you a blueprint to beat the bullies and teach you how to stand up, speak out, and reclaim your authority.

Let's face it, you cannot even turn on your television sets or scroll through an internet news feed without seeing a story where a child is bullied at school, an employee is intimidated in the workplace, or a government official uses a Twitter account to cyberbully the world using one of the coward's biggest tools—a computer.

In this innovative book, Bullseye The Clown™ gives a no-rubber-chickens-barred-approach to how he overcame bullies after many years of trial and error. This is his journey, and what worked for him may or may not be the best thing to work for you. One person's journey is not the cure for everyone. Just like one-size-fits-all underwear doesn't cover all the butts in the world.

The truth is, something drastic needs to be done to empower the bullied to take a stand and fight back in a way that is constructive, impactful, and maybe somewhat controversial. Although this book is written by a clown, what you are reading is not a love-your-enemies-hold-hands-and-sing-Kum-Ba-Yah kind of book. This is more of a love-yourself-so-bullies-don't-destroy-you-book.

Although the word bully is in the title, make no mistakes about it. This book is not about them. YOU are the star of this book. What **you** say goes. The time has come for you to rewrite your life story. How you decide to bully-proof your life is your decision. If you feel it's necessary to come face-to-face with your bully, try to work it out between you, and forgive them, then that is what you should do.

However, if you never want to see your bully again, that is perfectly okay as well. I will give you tips, stories, and nuggets to assist you along the way. Take what works for you, and cast aside the things that don't. You may find that what doesn't work for you at this precise moment might work for you two months down the road. Great! Wait until then to use it.

I dedicate this book to my father. My only regret is that I did not get it published before his passing. Thank you for your support, even though you did not know what I had been writing.

To my mother, for all the times you thought I was being antisocial, when in fact I was in my room writing and researching this book. (It's finally done. Can you believe it?)

I would also like to thank Tripp Burnett for all the fun illustrations in this book. Your ability to draw super fast is greatly appreciated.

Many thanks to Jan Bear, the Book Genie, for getting this book formatted, designing the layout, and getting this book uploaded. It couldn't have been done without you.

A super special thanks to Leslie Ann Akin for your undying support of this project. Thank you for believing in me, even when I didn't believe in myself. No one could ask for a better mentor and partner in crime!

Finally, I dedicate this book to you, the reader. May you finally find the courage to stand up to those who bully you, speak out for those who cannot yet speak for themselves, and reclaim the authority you have given away to the bullies.

Now is the time to take control!

~Bullseye The Clown™

To find more interesting information about overcoming bullies visit Bullseye The Clown™ at www.BullseyeTheClown.com

# Introduction

IF YOU LOOK BACK ON your life so far, or take a current snapshot of how your life is unfolding right now, are you as free-spirited as you should be, or do you feel you're being held hostage by your own life?

Have you ever walked into a room and, from the moment you entered, felt as though you didn't belong? Whether it's a classroom that you have to be a part of, an awards banquet you are more than qualified to take part in, or a work function that you are being paid to attend, no matter what reason you have for being there, you just feel out of place? Try as they might, no friend or family member's reassurances can do anything to make you feel welcome?

Or perhaps this scenario has a more familiar ring to it. From the moment you enter school, you seem to be the unpopular kid. Classmates make fun of you, call you names, steal your lunch money, hang your underwear up on the flagpole, or just have a complete general distaste for you. You are an outcast at work. Whether it's because you are younger than everyone, older, smarter, etc., and nothing you do can make your co-workers like you or invite you to parties.

Are you angry and defensive most of the time because of the way others have mistreated you? Do you feel lonely and depressed because you don't make friends easily? Have you avoided relationships for the fear of dating or getting hurt? Are you afraid of opening up to people because you expect rejection?

If any of these situations have ever happened to you or are currently happening, let me ask you a very serious question. What do you feel these classmates, co-workers, and so-called friends stole from you? Wait! What? Steal? "I didn't say they stole anything from me." Oh, but they have.

Some have stolen your joy. When is the last time you have seen your self-confidence? If you are going to be completely honest, some have stolen your future. Huh? You might ask yourself how someone can actually steal your future. It's simple.

Ask yourself, "Have I accomplished everything I had set out to do by this age?" If you said, "Yes," fantastic! You are thriving despite what those bullies did to you. However, if you answered "No," ask yourself, "What has kept me from achieving those goals?" I would say it's lack of self-confidence, or lack of belief, because of something someone told you, is one of the likely culprits.

When others bully or mistreat us, one of two things happens to us. Either we become super successful just to prove these bullies wrong, or we cannot reach our true potential because we buy into the malarkey that the bullies sold us.

---

*"You're looking at someone who would get the belt every day. Will you shut up, Susan! Whack! I was left behind at school because of one thing or another. I was a slow learner.*

*I was bullied at school because I had a slight disability and I was a bit slow. It hasn't really scarred me that much.*

*It was all psychological stuff. Some kids don't know they're being cruel. Some kids do and get a kick out of it. They could make me scream and bawl, and that made some of them "Whoo-hoo! Let's make her scream and bawl" because I was hyperactive.*

*It got physical as well. There was a lady at school who used to stub her cigarettes on me and bash me about and stuff, until one day I got fed up with it and gave her a pasting. I could fight back when I needed to. I give the impression I couldn't fight back. I could when I needed to.*

*She had nice long hair, this lassie. So, I just grabbed the hair and put her down. She didn't bother me after that."*

> — *Susan Boyle*
> *(Grammy-Award-nominated singer with more than 19 million albums sold worldwide)*

---

The best revenge you can get over any bully is success! Success means something different to everyone. Whether it's owning your own company, writing a book, recording an album, or simply being happy, proving that you survived despite the way others treated you is one of the most satisfying blows you can land on your bully.

This book is your resource for reclaiming everything that was taken from you, seeking your revenge, and empowering you to stand up and speak out from this point forward. Your bully-proof blueprint begins now.

# How to Use This Book

IF YOU PICKED UP THIS book and thought to yourself, "Why is this book so tiny?" then you are not alone. That was the entire purpose of this book. You are holding a pocket survival guide. I have provided you with a go-to guide for when bullying creeps up and you are not sure how to handle it. The idea is for you to just flip quickly to the chapter and get answers.

You will not find lengthy chapters or convoluted or complex diagrams. (Oh, wait, "convoluted" is a pretty complex word. What on earth does that mean?) What I was trying to say is, this book should be easy to follow. I took the bull out of bullying and left you with practical advice and options for combating bullying.

If there is something in this book that you cannot find or need help with, you can visit our website at www.BullseyeTheClown.com or email me at bullseye@BullseyeTheClown.com. I, Bullseye The Clown, will read and respond to all emails.

# Why Is this Book Written by a Clown?

THAT IS AN EXCELLENT QUESTION with a very simple answer. From the time I entered junior high school, I never fit in. I was too wimpy to fit in with the jocks. I wasn't smart enough to be a nerd. Although I was in choir, I could barely carry a tune without talented singers beside me, piping the right notes into my ears. Sometimes I opened my mouth, and the only voice heard was from the other singers.

During this time, I didn't stand up for myself. Bullies pushed me into lockers, called me names, and made fun of me. Getting into a fist fight was never my idea of fun, and I was always shy and rarely spoke up when bullies would mock me or say bad things about me. What I soon found out, however, is that I possessed something that many of the bullies did not—a quick wit!

When they called me names or bullied me, I cracked a joke or whipped a zinger at the bullies, and was soon (unintentionally) considered the class clown. This title, however, did not come without its own set of problems. Many times I would get caught talking in class and made to stand in the corner. I rarely minded this predicament, as this gave me a stage and a bigger audience to play to. After standing in the corner several times, the teachers realized that this added more fuel to the fire, and before long, they took away my stage, but by that time, it was too late. I was a clown.

The bullies created this clown, so it was only fitting that this clown write the book on how to shut the bullies down.

# Did You Know?

ACCORDING TO RESEARCH PUBLISHED IN the International Journal of Humor Research, class clowns may be the brightest kids in the room.

Their study reveals that humor ability and overall intelligence are tightly connected in middle school–aged children.

"We were particularly interested in the quality of humor made by children. Parents and teachers should know that if their children and students frequently make good quality humor, it is highly likely they have extraordinary intelligence," says lead study author and Anadolu University researcher Ugur Sak.

"Children use humor mostly for peer acceptance."

All this time I thought I might have a screw loose by becoming a clown. Turns out I am a genius!

## CHAPTER 1
# What Is Bullying?

IT IS IMPOSSIBLE TO GO any further in this book without first defining what "bullying" actually is. When you picked up this book, I am sure that you had a pretty clear understanding of what bullying means to you. However, as I coach individuals, I have found that there is a common trend where every bad behavior is lumped together under the umbrella of bullying, so it has become essential to create a definition of bullying for the sake of reference and to differentiate bullying from other types of abuse.

Bullying is unwanted, aggressive, and repetitive behavior intending to harm another individual. Bullying involves a real or perceived imbalance of power and can occur in many forms: verbal, social, physical, and cyber. The three key components you need to understand with bullying are these.

## Components of Bullying

**Repetition**

Bullying happens on more than one occasion. This is a recurring problem. Bullying may not always take the same form each time, but a bully will keep repeating the behavior until they feel they have control over you.

**Intent**

The primary intent of a bully is to harm, threaten, or control you. Their primary aim is not as a joke, but to overpower you.

**Power Imbalance (Real or Perceived)**

A bully will use his or her "real" or "perceived" power to exert dominance over you. This power balance can take many forms. Adults and teachers use their power over children. Some men try to abuse their power over women. The rich have used their wealth to control the poor.

Bosses rule over their company and often abuse their status to get their desired results. Those who are physically strong will prey on those who appear weaker. (I will discuss this further in the chapter "Power vs. Authority.")

## Types of Bullying

**Verbal bullying** is saying or writing malicious, hurtful, and many times dishonest things, which include name-calling, inappropriate sexual comments, taunting behavior to evoke a response, and threatening to cause bodily harm.

**Social bullying** is causing damage to someone's reputation or personal relationships. Leaving someone out on purpose, telling others not to be friends with someone, spreading rumors, and publicly embarrassing others fall under this category.

**Physical bullying** involves causing damage to a person, or a person's belongings. As the name implies, this type of bullying includes pinching, kicking, punching, spitting, pushing, tripping, and taking or breaking someone else's property.

**Cyber bullying** occurs behind the veil of the world wide web, taking place over digital devices such as computers, cell phones, and tablets. Cyber bullying can reach you through your social media accounts such as Facebook and Twitter, via text message, or in chat rooms (do these still exist?) and forums. The behavior most common to cyber bullying is sending, posting, or sharing negative, harmful, or misleading information about someone else. (I devoted a special chapter to cyber bullying.)

## What Bullying Is Not

Defining what makes up bullying is much easier than explaining what bullying is not. Many people do not consider many of the following items bullying. However, if abused and repeated, these can lead to bullying.

Conflict is an incompatibility between two or more people where the needs, wishes, opinions, and interests of each party are at odds. On the surface, having a conflict does not mean it's bullying. Proper conflict resolution techniques can definitely prevent bullying from happening.

Discipline is the practice of training people to obey rules or a code of behavior, using punishment to correct disobedience. Someone can take discipline too far, as we have witnessed with police brutality, and most times, they put the wrong people in charge of correcting behavior. Discipline is a necessary step when trying to correct behavior, and it can happen without bullying and abuse.

Teasing is a way to make fun of or attempt to provoke a person or animal in a playful way. If you are teasing someone, make sure the recipient is in on the jokes with you. If they are not, your behavior is borderline bullying. If they ask you to stop, and you do, it's teasing. However, if you continue to tease in an unwanted manner, it becomes bullying.

BRYAN LEE

## What to Do If You Think You Are Being Bullied

First thing, identify your bully by name. Put this in writing, do it now! List your bullies below. (Don't worry, you never have to show this list to anyone, unless you choose to.)

_____

_____

_____

_____

For each person you listed above, please write the type of behavior or aggression they are exuding against you (such as name-calling, hitting, punching, threatening, etc.). Include dates if you know them.

|  | **Date** |
|---|---|
|  |  |
|  |  |
|  |  |
|  |  |
|  |  |

List the intent of the actions, if you know, of each person. For example: My stepfather is hitting me in order to get me to clean my room. Is the intent to make you fearful, to make you give up a possession or money, threaten you, etc.?

_____

_____

_____

_____

Finally, are these incidents isolated? Or have they happened more than once? How often do they occur? Daily? Or do the bullies in question say that an action by you has caused them to treat you this way?

For example: My mother locks me in my room every time I refuse to do the dishes. (Circle one.)

| Once | More than Once | Daily |
| Once | More than Once | Daily |
| Once | More than Once | Daily |
| Once | More than Once | Daily |
| Once | More than Once | Daily |

Looking over your list above, if you circled once, more than likely that is not a bullying situation. Not that it isn't one, but bullying behavior is most often a repetitive offense.

Keep this list handy, as we will refer to it in later chapters.

## Chapter 2
# Why Are Bullies Targeting Me?

PERHAPS THE NUMBER ONE QUESTION I had on my mind when I was being bullied is, "Why are the bullies targeting me and not so-and-so?" Not that I had anything against so-and-so, and I definitely didn't want anyone else to be bullied, but I was just curious, "Why me?" There are a few reasons you are being targeted, so let's take a moment to explore them.

First, let it be said that although bullies seem tough and strong, they are complete cowards. How is that possible? If you notice, bullies never pick fights with people who are as strong or stronger than them. They seek people they perceive as weak, and they pick on them because they know a weaker target will not fight back.

# Reason 1

You appear physically weak to the bully. A bully could target you because you give off the impression you are weak and unable to fight back. Perhaps you walk with your head down. Are you quiet? Do you avoid eye contact with everyone?

There is *absolutely nothing wrong* with any of those actions. Being a quiet and polite person who minds their own business is quite the admirable quality. While a bully might mistake those qualities for weakness, they can also be your strength. We will talk more about this in the chapter, Your Body Speaks.

## Example

As a child, I was quiet and kept to myself. I did everything others asked me to do. I tried not to miss school, did my homework to the best of my ability, and did what I could to avoid trouble.

However, bullies still found me, called me names, pushed me into lockers, and tripped me whenever they could.

I never fought back. Instead, I started clowning around. Every time they came up to push me, I shouted, played dead, laughed, danced, and made a complete spectacle of myself. It scared the bejesus (and yes, that is an actual word in the clown world) out of them.

I think they thought I was a mental patient at the local nut house, and I didn't tell them any different.

They soon feared the unknown and left me alone. They never really knew what crazy thing I'd do next, and, honestly, I had no clue either. I made it up on the spot.

# Reason 2

You appear financially inferior to your bully. For some unknown reason, some people who have more money than others think they may belittle, name-call, and bully those who do not have as much money. This unfortunately happens more often than I would like to admit. I have seen it and witnessed it first hand frequently.

## Example

In high school, there was a girl named Joanna. She grew up on a farm, and before school, it was her duty to go out and feed all the farm animals. After a full day at school, Joanna would then go home, feed the animals again, do many chores around the farm, then retire to her room at dark to work on her homework. Often, Joanna would get on the school bus looking exhausted and smelling like the farm she worked so hard to maintain.

Her classmates used to poke fun at her, call her names, and tell her she smelled like a pig. None of them were aware of how hard Joanna worked on that farm, how dedicated she was to the farm animals, and how much joy the farm brought her. No one cared to ask or get to know her.

Most of the ones bullying Joanna had no after-school job. Their parents were wealthy, instilling in their children that work is of no value to their kids. The rich kids received money from their parents without having to do anything to earn it. On the surface, it would appear as though rich people were lazy, mean bullies, as if the world owed them something for nothing.

Just as those classmates of Joanna's assumed that she was inferior because she worked, Joanna's friends assumed the complete opposite of the bullies. Just as no two boys are the same, no two girls are the same. We can say that no two rich people or poor people are the same. Assume nothing based on previous experience.

## REASON 3

Bullies perceive you as an outcast. In case you're wondering what exactly that is, an outcast is rejected, or cast out. This outcast can be from home or society, excluded, looked down upon, or ignored. Basically, anyone who does not fit in with normal society, if there is even such a thing as a normal society.

So, what causes people to become an outcast? Physical appearances or physical disabilities, perceived developmental disorders, even brain diseases such as alcoholism can be factors for making one feel like an outcast. Many times, when people don't understand a disease or a condition, they fear it. This fear drives people away and can make the outcast feel isolated and withdrawn.

## Example

Perhaps one group of people who seem to be outcasts more than others is the homeless. We see them every day and on the street corners, under bridges, or standing outside grocery stores and gas stations. Most of the time, we simply ignore them. No one ever says hello to them or sits and talks with them. No one ever investigates or cares to ask them what circumstances led them to be homeless.

Instead, people sneer at them, look away when they approach, and even call them names and kick them as they walk by. I find the whole homeless situation very sad, because we are all one big catastrophe away from being homeless. What if your house caught on fire, you lost your job, and you had no money? What would you do?

# Reason 4

You are a member of a minority group. What does this mean? This means that a bully could target you because of your race, sexual orientation, gender, or religion. Honestly, some bullies don't even need a reason to bully you. They do it for the power trip they get from it.

## Example

From the moment The CW announced that actress Ruby Rose would portray Batwoman in their upcoming series, cyberbullies went into a frenzy, ripping her to shreds. Twitter users went crazy saying that Rose, who is a lesbian, was not good enough to play the first openly gay superhero, and that she wasn't fit for the role because she wasn't actually Jewish.

Gay men and lesbians even bullied her, who did not feel that she was lesbian enough. To take a stand against those who were bullying her, she shut down her Twitter account and disabled the comments on her Instagram account. But she even took time out to address the hypocrisy of her haters.

Bryan Lee

Ruby Rose tweeted, "Where on earth did 'Ruby is not a lesbian, therefore she can't be Batwoman' come from—has to be the funniest, most ridiculous thing I've ever read. I came out at 12? And have for the past five years had to deal with 'she's too gay' how do y'all flip it like that? I didn't change."

## Chapter 3
# Power vs. Authority

THE MOMENT WE'RE BORN, WE are each given two things: personal power and authority.

Personal power is gained over the course of our development and based on our strength and confidence. Although this is something we possess, many of us do not use it, don't know how to access it, or do not even know we have it.

If you look around, you'll see people walking around who seem incredibly powerful. Politicians, lawyers, doctors, and CEOs all walk in power. They exude confidence and charisma the moment they walk into a room. Are they more powerful than you?

You are just as powerful as any billionaire or any business leader. It's true. Although all those people have the same personal power that you have, they have something else that you might not possess, and that is positional power.

Positional power refers to the power or authority that is given to someone related to their rank or position in a company or organization. The CEO in a company has more power than a branch manager, for example. We have given teachers power over their students, but they answer to the principal and administration.

This power is related to their position and could be lost if they are fired, moved, or demoted into a different position.

Regardless of what personal or positional power another person possesses, there is one thing that they do **not** have over you, and that is authority.

Now there are definitely those who believe they have the authority to boss you around, mistreat you, call you names, and even push you around. But since they don't own you, as it is illegal to own another person, the only authority they have over you is the authority you give them.

How do we give our authority away?

- By not speaking up when someone bullies and mistreats us.

- By doing whatever the bully asks, whether we believe it is the right thing to do or not. If you believe it is wrong, and it's physically or mentally harmful to you, don't do it.

- By avoiding social situations because you know the bully will be there. This could include dances, movies, award ceremonies, etc. Never allow someone else to dictate how much fun you have.

- By complaining about bullying. This differs from telling someone about the bully. Once you have told someone, the more time you spend complaining and talking about them, the more power they will continue to have over you. Do not give the bully the satisfaction of knowing that they are still taking up space in your head.

- By allowing the bully to dictate what kind of day you're going to have. What does that mean? Well, the bully's intent is to make you fearful and upset. If you make it a goal to be happy despite what the bully does to you, you take away the hold that the bully has over you.

- By changing your dreams and plans because of what bullies tell you. Perhaps you dream of being a cheerleader. A bully laughs and says you would do a terrible job, so you abandon that dream. The bully won. Stop giving in to other people's expectations of what they think you are capable of.

**Great news!** No matter how much power and authority you have given away to a bully, you can take it back! I hope the reason you bought this book is to stand up and reclaim your authority.

## CHAPTER 4
# Fact or Myth: If I Tell Someone, the Bullying Will Stop

IF YOU CONSULT ANY OTHER book or website on bullying, one of the first tips you will more than likely see is tell someone you are being bullied. This could be a parent, friend, teacher, guidance counselor, supervisor at work, human resources, or even a coach if you are on a ball team. Although this is fairly sound advice, I am going to have to disagree on this one.

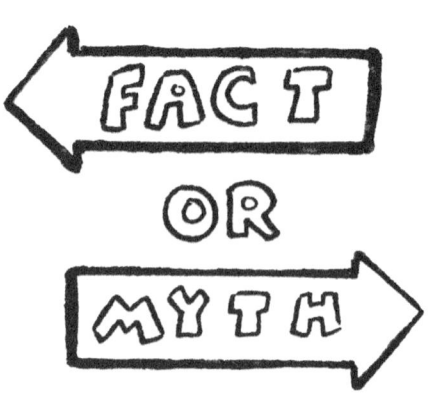

## MY EXPERIENCE OF REPORTING BULLYING

No one cares more about you being bullied than **you** do!

The moment people know you are being bullied, they will meet you with statements such as:

- "Perhaps he or she wasn't bullying you, but just having a bad day."
- "Did you say anything to upset or provoke them?"

- "Do your best to avoid them."
- "Just ignore them; they are harmless."
- "It's just a phase he or she is going through. They will grow out of it."
- "Can't you just try to get along?"

Not to say that your family, friends, and teachers don't believe you or don't care. It's just that they are unaware of the severity of the situation because they are not there to witness it.

Understand that it is completely possible, once you tell someone, and it is brought to the attention of others, including the bully, the bullying may continue or even get worse. It may anger the bully that you called them out or told on them, and they may want to take that out on you.

There is also a good likelihood that even though you tell teachers or supervisors about the situation, nothing happens at all. The teacher or supervisor may not want to cause a scene and simply dismiss your bullying claim. Perhaps the teacher or supervisor is friends with the bully or the bully's family. Whatever the reason, realize that nothing may change.

Therefore, you need to take matters into your own hands if no one helps you.

## What Happened When You Reported Bullying?

### Who Did You Tell and When?

Referring to Chapter 1, for each bullying occurrence you listed, write the name and date of the person you told. If you didn't tell anyone about it, just leave this section blank. For instance, if you told your math teacher that you were being bullied, write his or her name and when you told them.

|  | **Date** |
|---|---|
|  |  |
|  |  |
|  |  |

|  | **Date** |
|---|---|
|  |  |
|  |  |

## How Was the Bullying Incident Resolved?

Finally, how was each bullying incident resolved? Was the bully disciplined? Suspended? Was nothing done at all? Were the bully's parents called? Please list the resolution below. If no one helped you, simply write Nothing in the space provided.

_____

_____

_____

_____

_____

Now that you have these lists compiled, here are a few options for using them.

# How to Use Your Experiencee of Reporting Bullying

## Option 1

If the bullying issues are resolved, you can simply keep these lists for your records and do nothing.

## Option 2

If none of the bullying issues are resolved, take these to your school principal, human resources department, team coach, or whoever is in charge of your school, business, or organization. Ask them if they have a Bully-Proof Blueprint in place. If they are completely clueless, refer them to www.BullseyeTheClown.com/Blueprint. Show them your lists and ask them what the best course of action is to address the situation.

## Option 3

If Option 2 doesn't work, then it's apparent that the school or organization has no intention of helping resolve the situation. It has now become time for further help. If you are underage, inform your parents, and insist they act by contacting an attorney, or informing the news media. If that sounds too daunting a task, simply go to www.BullseyeTheClown.com/Complaint and file a complaint about your school and organization, and we will follow up with the school or organization on your behalf.

## Inaction

Inaction is not an option when it comes to bullying.

## CHAPTER 5
# The 3 Bs of a Bullying Situation

THE MOMENT A BULLYING INCIDENT occurs, there are basically three different roles we find ourselves cast in. Each role carries a particular responsibility, so knowing which category you fall into will assist you with deciding what your course of action should be. Those three roles are: (1) the Bully, (2) the Bullied, and (3) the Bystander.

## THE BULLY

The bully is the one who sets this ball in motion. His or her ill-conceived choice to start a war of words or a physical fight rests solely on the shoulders of the bully. There is always a choice whether to fight to take flight. The bully chooses his or her victim and sets the plan into motion.

## THE BULLIED

The second B of a bullying situation is the victim, and the one being bullied. From the moment the bully starts the attack (whether verbal or physical), the Bullied has to figure out whether to retreat, fight back, or call for help.

## The Bystander

The third B of a bullying situation is that of the bystander. The Bystander is a person who is present during a bullying event or incident but does not take part in it. Although the bullying situation doesn't involve the bystander, the bystander still has three, or sometimes four, very important decisions to make.

### Do Nothing

The bystander could decide to do nothing. Since they are in the wrong place when this incident occurs, they can simply choose to mind their own business and walk away.

### Intervene

The bystander could choose to help the one being bullied by stepping in and offering his or her to help. A majority of the time, however, this is not what the bystander does.

### Call For Help

The final decision a bystander could make is call for help. Whether it's calling 911 or seeking the aid of a police officer, teacher, or security guard, the best decision a bystander can make is to call for help.

### Join in

Unfortunately, on certain occasions, bystanders may join in on the bullying. Now why on earth would they do this? If they are friends with the bully, they might do it to maintain their friendship. If they are not really friends with the bully, perhaps they fear the bully will turn his or her attention to them. They feel that the best way to keep the bully at bay is to join in.

If you find yourself a bystander in a bullying situation, it is my opinion that you have a humanitarian duty to intervene. You should not put yourself in harm's way by trying to subdue a bully yourself, but you can call for help. Everyone seems to have a cell phone these days, so if you see someone in distress, call for help or leave the situation and find someone who can offer help like a teacher, co-worker, or police officer.

Many states have Good Samaritan Laws that offer limited protections to those who attempt to help a person in distress. These laws encouraged bystanders to get involved in emergency situations without fear of being sued if their actions inadvertently contributed to a person's injury or death.

## CHAPTER 6
# Don't Be a Bully for Your Cause

WE ALL HAVE A PASSION for something. Whether it's music, sports, or bug collecting, there is that one special thing that lights a fire in each one of us. No matter what that special thing is, not only do we want to spread the joy of it to friends and family, there is always someone out there who will disagree with you and tell you it's stupid.

Although it's wonderful to have a cause that you want to share with others, are your enthusiasm and how you share your views alienating the ones you are trying to convince to support your cause? How you approach others can have the opposite effect on them and, sometimes, it can seem like you are bullying them into sharing your point of view.

Can you believe that even clowns get bullied? You might think clowns are the happiest people on the planet, but even they can get bullied, and even by other clowns. It's an unfortunate fact that many people are becoming a bully for their own cause.

I recently observed a Facebook post from a well-respected clown who stated that "Clowns are only to perform for children. If you are not performing for children, you are not a real clown." A statement like this is purely opinion and not fact. For as far back as history goes, clowns, fools, and jesters were a common part of society and mainly played for adult audiences.

When I expressed these opinions on Facebook to a friend who ranted that everyone needs to perform for children and dress a certain way, I was told that because I didn't agree with her, she could not listen to anything I had to say. That, my friends, is a bully. Someone that only wants you to hear their side, and if you don't, will not listen to you, exhibits not only childish behavior, but bullying behavior. This is behavior that I made a point of calling out, and behavior I will not tolerate. Her point and her position now suffer because she is a clown bully.

The purpose of this chapter is neither to pass judgment on others or, the causes they believe in, nor to take away their joy or opinions. The sole purpose here is to educate anyone who speaks for a cause or believes in a cause, to take a moment, to see exactly how you represent that cause. Are your actions congruent with the mission of the cause, and are you open to two-way discussions on the issues, or do you bully everyone to take in your view?

There are already too many bullies in the world. Don't become another one.

Keep your joy and enthusiasm and be the change you want to see in the world.

## Chapter 7
# Elder Abuse: Are Your Parents Safe?

WHEN YOU PICKED UP a copy of this book, I bet you never thought you would hear me say this, but your parents may not be safe from bullies. Let me explain.

For many of us with aging parents, there is always that fear we may no longer be able to care for them at home. When that happens, looking for a nursing home or an assisted living facility can be a daunting task. We face a barrage of decisions all at once.

What does it cost? How nice are the rooms? Are there doctors and nurses on staff? Does insurance or Medicare cover any portion of the costs? Perhaps the one thought that never crosses our mind is, "Will my parents be safe here?"

Depending on the location of the facility, you might be a little leery because it's in a seedy part of town. Although the fear of a break-in or robbery might be a genuine concern, that is not exactly what I mean by being safe.

While cost and location may be extremely important when deciding where to place your parents, the most important question you should ask yourself is, "Who am I leaving my parents with?"

Many people will come into contact with your parents every day. I think it's incredibly important to know who exactly those people are.

Doctors, nurses, and caregivers are the first group of people who will interact with your parents daily. It would be very beneficial to meet as many of them as possible before deciding to entrust them with your own family. Are they friendly, knowledgeable, and someone you would enjoy spending your time with? If not, perhaps it's not the best idea to leave the ones you love into their care. Of course, it may not be possible to meet many of the staff, depending on how much time you actually have before making your decision.

So, the best people to ask are: Residents and neighbors. Meet as many of the residents who live in the facility as possible. Ask them questions about their neighbors and the staff to get an overall view of how happy the residents are where they are.

The first few questions that might go through your head right now are: "Why do I have to put so much energy and effort into finding out if my parents are going to be safe in a nursing home or assisted living facility? What could go wrong?" To answer those questions as simply as possible, many things could go wrong. That's not to say that they will go wrong;, but be aware that they could. Below is a brief list of what to look for.

**Physical abuse**—This is self-explanatory but could definitely include, hitting, punching, slapping, pinching, burning, pushing, restraining, kicking, false imprisonment or confinement (locking them in their room), over medicating, or even withholding medication as a means of punishment.

**Emotional or psychological abuse**—Humiliation is a tactic some places employ in order to get their residents to comply. This can range from yelling, name-calling, ridiculing, constantly criticizing, accusations, or blaming. It can also include finding out what is important to the older person, and withholding that until they comply with the demands of the worker.

This is not a definitive list of what could go wrong but gives you a starting point in what to look for when visiting your parents, whether they are being cared for in their own home, or a nursing home. So, what can we do to help minimize the amount of abuse heaped upon the elders in your life?

1. **Frequent visits.** Visiting frequently can make you more aware of what is going on. Always check for bruises, how your parents react when certain nurses and caregivers come into the room, talk to your parents, etc. For those of you who can't visit often because you don't live in the same city or state as your parents, see if there are any family friends around who can check in on them from time to time.

2. **Question the questionable.** If something doesn't look right (for example, bruises, scars, broken bones, wrist burns), ask questions. Ask your parents what happened and also check with a variety of staff.

3. **Investigate all complaints.** If your parents are complaining about things happening to them, believe them, and investigate. Perhaps the biggest problem occurs if your parents have dementia, and they report something to you, and you have no way of knowing if what they are reporting is real. Again, watch how they react to certain workers and other residents. Monitor bruises, broken bones, etc. When people are on blood thinners, they bruise easily.

4. **Know what medications your parents take.** Knowing what medications your parents are taking, and the side effects can be very beneficial. This information will be beneficial in knowing if your parents are over medicated, under medicated, if their medications are being withheld, etc.

5. **Have one specific person in charge of their finances.** To avoid theft of money from your parents, it's not a good idea to give over one person access to cash, credit cards, or checking

accounts. Putting one person in charge of the finances is best. Likewise, keep very little to no cash on hand. If your parents still have control over their own finances, make sure they keep checkbooks, cash and credit cards in a secure location.

6. **Be aware of drastic changes in mood or health.** If your parents have always been happy, carefree people, and suddenly become mean, overly paranoid, or withdrawn, this could be a sign that something else could go on with them. Also, if they have a drastic change in their health, or quality of life, make sure you ask lots of questions and don't just accept things at face value.

7. **Record it.** If you fear your parents are being abused, and cannot seem to find the answers you are looking for, install a hidden camera somewhere in their room—one you can monitor using your cell phone. This is not designed to catch someone in the act; it is to ensure that your parents are safe.

8. **Watch their interaction with staff and nurses.** A real sign something could be wrong is to watch how your parents act when staff and nurses enter the room. Are they smiling and chatting? Do they stiffen up and look scared? Although both traits may not actually show that something is wrong, it might be a great way to start a dialogue with your parents once they leave the room. "That nurse seems really nice," and see where the conversation leads.

Although it's a topic that no one really wants to bring up or discuss, keeping an open communication with not only your parents, but staff and residents is a great way to ensure the safety of your parents when you are not around. Do not be afraid to ask questions. If you are afraid to ask questions, that is a sign something is wrong.

# The Survival Tips

## CHAPTER 8
# How to Counterattack a Bully

Now that we have spent some time defining what bullying is and isn't, it's time to find out how to counter the bully and beat him or her at their own game.

The two key topics I would like to discuss in this chapter are how to avoid the bully and what to do when you come face to face with the bully.

### How to Avoid the Bully

Do not give the bully the chance to pounce. If you work with a bully, try to arrange your schedule to avoid working at the same time or in the same place as the bully. If the bully targets you at lunch, go to lunch at a different time. If the bully targets you in the hallway at school, change your path to keep the bully guessing where you are. If the bully has trouble finding you, he or she will slowly lose interest.

Travel in packs. If you can find a buddy at work, on your team or in your classes, hang out as long as possible with him or her. If you don't have a buddy, and you see another loner who is being bullied also, offer to be a friend or a buddy. There is strength in numbers, and bullies are less likely to attack a group.

Stand up and don't back down. When you are afraid of another person, or feel somewhat inferior to them, it probably seems impossible to stand your ground because you are not feeling brave. Being strong does not mean that you are not afraid. It just means that you sometimes have to **do it afraid!**

Find someone that you think is brave, or who can stand up to anyone, and watch them. How do they stand? How do they walk? What do they say when they talk? If you have to practice being strong at home, then do it, so that when you encounter your bully, you will implement it. (Check out the next chapter, "How to Keep Bullies from Targeting You.")

Be strong to feel strong! One of the best ways that you can be strong in the face of fear is to feel strong. Work out, lift weights, run, or do whatever makes you feel strong. Take a self-defense class, karate, Zumba, whatever, just do things that make you feel better about yourself, and things that make you feel ready to conquer the world!

Pre-script a response. If your palms get sweaty and you feel you are getting ready to vomit when you see the bully out of the corner of your eye, a great way to get prepared for this meeting is by pre-planning.

Most bullies are unoriginal and usually say the same mean things over and over. If you know their usual remarks, sit down and create a clever response. That way, when you encounter the bully, it will equip you.

This is something I did when I was a stand-up comedian and playing in comedy clubs. I wrote jokes just in case someone yelled at me from the audience. This is a very empowering tool to have in your arsenal. For more information on how to pre-script your responses, please visit www.BullseyeTheClown.com/prescript

## What to Do When You Come Face to Face with a Bully

### Speak Out

If a bully approaches you and verbally or physically attacks, stand up for yourself and speak out. Audibly alert everyone around you by shouting "No! Back Off!"

## Do Not Give Any of Your Authority Away

Tell the bully they have no authority over you and their behavior is inappropriate.

## Do Not Become a Bully

A natural reaction when someone strikes you or verbally attacks is to attack back.

## Do Not Call the Bully Names

Do not engage in a physical altercation with the bully unless you are defending yourself.

## Stay Calm

Do not show the bully that they upset you. Chances are, you are going to be upset, but bullies thrive on knowing that they can get you angry. Stay calm, stand your ground, and speak your mind, but do it calmly.

## Report It!

If someone is bullying you at work, tell a supervisor or take it to your Human Services Department. If you are on a sports team, report the bullying to your coach. If it's your coach who is doing the bullying, report it to his superiors. If it's a parent, report it to a teacher or school counselor.

## Record It!

Catch the bully's behavior on video. Whether it's recorded on a cell phone, body cam, or some other device, it's very difficult for a bully to deny what is on video.

Do not put yourself in harm's way just to capture a video!

If you cannot safely capture it, please don't attempt it. If you see anyone around you filming it, ask them for a copy of the video. (What do you do with this video once you have it? Refer to the chapter titled "Is Publicly Shaming a Bully Bullying?")

## Cause a Distraction

As I mentioned earlier in the book, when bullies came after me at school, I would do many things that would cause a commotion. I screamed fire, jumped up and down, and played dead. Do anything that might seem unexpected to the bully to cause panic and uncertainty. If you do this every time they approach you, the bullies will think twice before causing more attention.

## WHAT TO DO IF YOU ENCOUNTER A CYBER BULLY ONLINE

Research every friend request **before** you accept it. The moment someone sends you a friend request on Facebook, before you even click the accept button, you have the chance to check out the potential friend's profile. Always check out their profile before you accept them as a friend.

What are you looking for? You are looking to see what they post. Are they positive and encouraging? Do they seem like friends you would want to hang out with? Or do they spend most of their time posting negative comments and calling people names?

Chances are, the way they react on their own profile is the way they will react to yours. You have authority to say who is your Facebook friend. Choose them wisely.

Respond nicely. If someone leaves a negative comment on any of my social media channels, I usually will respond the **first** time. I thank them for taking the time to leave me a message.

Address their issue nicely, and once again thank them for their time. If they continue writing mean things . . . , delete or unfriend them. There is great power in blocking, deleting and unfriending those who cyber bully you. Always remember, your social media pages are **yours!**

Nobody else can tell you what friend you have to accept and who you can delete. If people are making your social media time a negative experience, get rid of them.

Keep a record. Always keep a hard copy of all the bullying posts. That way, if the bully continues trying to bully you on other social media channels or through email, you will have a journal that you can show adults, coworkers, teachers, or the police if need be.

Report it! Chances are if a bully is threatening you or name calling online, they are going against that website's terms of use. There is usually a way to report posts and comments as hate speech, bullying or harassment. Most websites and social media platforms will delete comments and close users' accounts if they continue violating their bullying policies.

Do **not** call the bully names. Under no circumstance should you stoop to the bully's level and name-call or get even with them. This will only make the bullying worse. Simply block or delete them.

Never open messages from people you don't know. If you get a message and texts from people you don't know, delete them. Many of these texts, emails and messages contain viruses and can harm your computer.

Stand up for your friends. Even if you are not the one who is being bullied online, but your friends are, you can still help. If you don't feel safe enough telling the bully to leave your friend alone, then take a screenshot of the incident and report it! Let's not only stand up for ourselves, but for others.

CHAPTER 9
# How to Keep Bullies from Targeting You: Your Body Speaks

IN CHAPTER 2 WE WENT into detail about why bullies may target you, which leads us to the following question: Is there anything I can do to keep bullies from targeting me?

The short answer is "Yes!" However, keep in mind that what I am about to share with you may take some time for you to feel comfortable implementing. It may take time for the bullies to notice that something is a little different with you.

If you recall, one reason bullies may target you is because you may appear physically and mentally weaker, and the bully always feels confident knowing that he or she can dominate you.

Here are a few survival tips you can incorporate into your daily routine that will make bullies think twice before messing with you.

Even without uttering one word to your bully, your body can speak volumes. Do you walk with your head lowered? Do you avoid eye contact? Are you always looking at your phone? Are you shy? Quiet? Reserved? Do you walk slumped over?

Although there is nothing wrong with any of those actions, this type of body language and posture sends messages to potential bullies that you lack confidence and can make you one of their targets.

Let's give your body language a fresh voice!

## How To Improve Your Body Language

Make eye contact with everyone when you walk. Instead of keeping your head down and looking at the floor while you are walking, keep your eyes focused on everyone! This is key for two very important reasons. First, monitoring your surroundings will alert you when a bully comes your way. Second, maintaining eye contact with your peers shows you are confident and unafraid. (You might be afraid, but to others you appear confident and that is half the battle when dealing with a bully.)

Stand up straight and do not slump your shoulders. When you slump your shoulders and stoop over when you walk, not only can you not see where you are going, but this gives bullies the impression that you are weak. Instead, stand up straight when you walk. Puff out your chest a little. If you are not sure how to do this, watch movies or television shows of your favorite hero or heroine and mimic the way they walk. You might feel silly at first, but soon you will command attention when you walk in the room for the right reasons!

Do **not** fold your arms across your chest. When you come face to face with a bully, notice where the bully's hands are. Mirror the images of the bully. Stand the same way he or she is. Through body language, show the bully that you are not afraid.

Stand with your feet shoulder width apart. A wider stance like this will ground your body and make it more difficult for a bully to knock you down. The closer your feet are together and the more closed off your body is, if a bully bumps into you, the easier it is to knock you off balance.

## How to Speak with Power

Use a strong, confident voice. Do not whisper as that shows signs of weakness, but do not yell at a bully as that might make the bully more aggressive. Use a forceful and confident voice.

Use phrases like, "You have no authority over me," or "This is inappropriate behavior." Simply tell them to "Stop." Do not threaten them.

Walk with a purpose. When walking the halls at school or work, walk with a purpose. Stay focused on getting to your destination without wasting time by checking your text messages. You can check your phone when you arrive.

For more in-depth ways to make your body speak a distinctive language, please visit www.Bullseyetheclown.com/YourBodySpeaks.

## CHAPTER 10
# Workplace Bullying

MANY PEOPLE THINK BULLYING ONLY happens to children in school or young adults in college. Bullying happens **everywhere**, even in the workplace. It would probably surprise most children to learn that their parents have the potential to be bullied or be a bully at work.

### WHAT IS WORKPLACE BULLYING?

What is bullying in the workplace? Below is a short list of ways adults are bullied while they are at work.

- Inappropriate jokes or mocking an employee
- Overly harsh criticism of an employee
- Not allowing an employee to take time off for a vacation or illness
- Pressuring an employee to work overtime and set unrealistic goals for them to reach
- Excessive supervision that implies the employee is performing poorly

- Excluding specific employees from company functions and parties
- Taking credit for another employee's work
- Retaliation for standing up to a bully
- Talking about employees behind their back
- Spreading rumors about employees

## What Should I Do If I Am Being Bullied at Work?

**Document it.** The first thing you should do is to make sure you document everything that happens to you and keep a log or a journal. In order to ensure that something gets done about workplace bullying, you may need to prove it is an ongoing problem and not an isolated incident.

**Report it.** Report the incident to your supervisor or your Human Resources Department. If it is your supervisor who is the bully, then you will have to report it to HR. If nothing gets done at either of those levels, try to contact the owner or CEO of the business and let them know what is going on.

**Speak up immediately.** Don't wait until the bullying gets too far out of hand. At the first sign of trouble, make sure you call out the bully and make them aware that you will not be tolerating this behavior.

**Consult your employee handbook.** Some companies have a policy on bullying and workplace harassment. Check your handbook for this policy and follow the steps listed in your handbook. If your company doesn't have a specific policy for that, direct them to www.BullseyeTheClown.com/Blueprint and we can help create a Bully-Proof Blueprint for them.

## CHAPTER 11
# Is Publicly Shaming a Bully Bullying?

THERE SEEMS TO BE A trend currently exploding on social media these days called cancel culture. If an internet user doesn't like something that you say, or gets offended by something that you do, they work tirelessly to get you fired from your job, and try to get your own friends and followers to turn on you.

This phenomenon is nothing new. It dates back centuries and known as public shaming and public humiliation. Public shaming is punishment whose major feature is dishonoring or disgracing a person, usually an offender or prisoner, in a public setting.

Question: Is publicly shaming bullying?

This is a topic that many people cannot agree on and, as I attempt to offer a solution, you will soon discover that there are many answers to this question.

We should consider many factors before ever trying to put a public shaming into action.

First, no one should experience public shaming because of a belief they hold. Whether it's their religion, their belief in doctors and vaccines, or even what political party they choose. We all have beliefs in different things, and regardless of what others say, you do not have to believe what someone else believes. If they try to shame you for that, that is bullying.

Freedom of speech is a right given to us in the United States Constitution. Therefore, we may say whatever we wish, even if it offends someone. We should not use words for harm and should never tell lies about people. Someone should never publicly shame us for something we have said. Hate speech, however, is a different matter.

What is the difference between free speech and hate speech?

Free speech or freedom of speech allows people to share their beliefs, thoughts, and ideas openly. It presents two sides of an issue and encourages debate. It can improve society through social change and generally gets supported. Free speech protects and values minorities and is humane in nature.

Hate speech, on the other hand, incites violence against others. It does not encourage healthy debate, but violence. Hate speech is degrading to society and hurts others while getting socially punished. Hate speech is inhumane and shows prejudice to different minority groups. This type of speech is immoral.

All throughout this book, a survival tip that I have given over and over is to get your bully on camera, if possible. Once you have footage of a bullying incident, what should you do with it? If you post it online, is that considered public shaming?

Here is where my answer to this question may vary from other experts. I have maintained and will always maintain the viewpoint that . . .

Calling and speaking out against a bully is not bullying!

The video footage that you have collected of your bully is not so much public shaming as it is public informing. You can post videos of your bully online without calling them names, without telling lies and untruths about them, and with little or no commentary.

The video should speak for itself. If the bully is feeling shamed by a video of the incident being posted, the only person he or she has to blame is himself or herself. If their own behavior embarrasses them, it should. Perhaps once their friends, family and coworkers see their behavior, the bully will change his or her conduct.

As someone who has been bullied over and over, I wish I had a social media platform back when I was getting bullied. We didn't have the internet back when I was a kid. We didn't have Twitter and cyber bullies.

Back in my day, the bullies made house calls. They showed up on our front lawn, lit bags of cow patties on fire, and threw them on our porch. (If you don't know what a cow patty is, try googling it!)

I hold little sympathy for bullies. Not only do I think it is essential to expose them, it is a public service. The sooner we can stop a bully, the safer the public will be.

Stand up and speak out against bullies, and inform the public if you run into a bully. You just might save someone from becoming the next bullying victim.

## CHAPTER 12
# Letter from a Bully

EVERY ONCE IN A WHILE, a bully may recognize the pain and discomfort he or she may have caused you, and try to reach out to apologize or make amends. This actually happened to me, and I wanted to include this letter and some additional correspondence with the bully, just to give you a brief insight why some bullies bully.

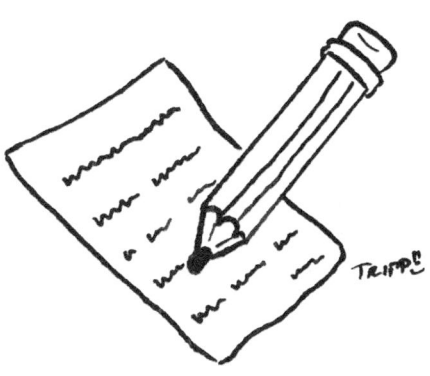

*Dear Bullseye,*

*We went to the same school, a long time ago. I found myself confronted with having offended/hurt classmates feelings recently. Shocking, I know. Anyway, that made me want to apologize to the people that I know that I was mean to. You came to mind. I apologize for my small-minded younger self. This may seem random and out of the blue.*

*"I'm sorry" and I hope you are and remain well.*

*So long as you understand that I'm trying to explain and not make excuses. You may not recall but I moved to the area in 2nd grade. This school was my 5th school* *that school year. I may have been imagining things, but I didn't fit in well. I always thought that was because I was mixed race. We were not poor, but my father was a greedy cheap a\*\*. So I became embarrassed by my clothes, bagged lunch and overall lack of finances.*

*All of that being said, I feel I was mean to people to fit in with the wrong crowd. Either following their lead or being mean to gain favor from whomever.*

*In junior high and high school I think I got better. In fact, I became friends with some that would be considered outsiders. At that point, I think my personality would be the reason people thought I was mean or the reason I was actually mean.*

*I did a few stints in a psych ward while in school. Everything from depression to bi-polar was written in my charts. This fact actually helped me get kicked out of high school and the Navy. I rejected those diagnoses then and now. What I do cop to is being a narcissistic borderline personality.*

*Basically, I am not a pleasant person. I am hyper critical and generally pessimistic. So while there is usually truth in what I say, it is often ignored because it comes across as just being mean.*

*This is all I got. I had no reasons to be mean. I am generally not mean, just an a\*\*hole sometimes.*

*Best of luck with your book, if I can be of any help, let me know.*

*Signed,*
*Your Bully*

---

After receiving this letter, I drafted my response to the bully to see if I could shed some light on why he thought he was so mean. Was he being mean to me and others because some people were being mean to him?

This was his response.

> *I wouldn't make that connection, but yes, lots of folks were mean to me. I was called an oreo, half-breed, the N word, you name it. Not only by the kids, but many more parents.*
>
> *Some of my neighbors liked playing with me, but their parents didn't like them associating with me . . . but I don't recall seeking out people to take revenge on. If that were the case, I think I would have confronted them. I was in plenty of fights with kids who were not nice to me.*

I wanted to know if his bullying behavior had any effect on his current life. Or did he completely out-grow his mean tendencies? Below is his final response.

> *The few relationships I have had ended badly. To some degree because I am sort of an a\*\*. My relationships with my family are mostly strained because I am sort of an a\*\*. I work a solitary job because I grew tired of working with and for people that I could not respect/stand. I have been able to control myself to a degree at work though.*
>
> *I work my current decision by choice. Today, I am a person with very strong opinions, who is generally not afraid to express them. However, I mostly keep to myself because I am aware that most people do not share in my beliefs.*
>
> *From time to time, I still say something kind of crazy and hurt someone's feelings. Thankfully it isn't based on things such as sexual orientation, skin color or body type.*

I will admit, that after reading this letter and the responses to my questions a few times, the bully's answers made me a little sad. As a bully, he has never really been able to rise above the hurt and anger and actually thrive.

He lives a solitary life, with strained relationships and if you read closely, doesn't seem to have much joy in his life.

Sound familiar?

Many of us who were bullied have been living the same life.

## Are You a Bully?

Do you fear you might be a bully or have bullying tendencies? Do you think your child might be a bully? Here are a few questions to ask yourself or someone you may suspect of being a bully.

- Do you hurt other people on purpose?

- Do you send mean, disrespectful, and threatening messages on social media platforms, by text, or through email?

- Do you call people names?

- Do you ignore friends, family members, classmates, and co-workers, or avoid inviting them to events and parties on purpose, just to make them feel bad?

- Do you spread rumors about others, whether the rumors are true?

- Do you tease other people based on how they dress or what they look like?

- Do you try to make other people afraid of you?

- Do you push, shove, hit, or pinch others just to get a reaction out of them?

- Do you laugh at other people's misfortune?

- Do you try to steal or destroy other people's property?

If you answered yes to any of these questions, chances are you are probably a bully. Although this book is titled Your Blueprint to Beating the Bullies, here are a few tips to prevent or rehabilitate a bully.

## Survival Tips for a Bully

Find an outlet for your hostility and anger. If you find you are getting angry and upset a lot by other people, find a different outlet instead of becoming a bully. Paint, draw, play a sport, or learn to play a musical instrument. Find a hobby that you enjoy spending your time and energy on.

Compliment someone every day. Find someone throughout your day that you can pay a compliment. Whether it's "Nice shirt," or "I like your shoes," or "You look wonderful in that shade of blue." an easy way to make new friends, or get others to like you, is to pay them compliments.

Do something nice for others. If someone falls, help them up. Say hello to a homeless person on the street and offer to get them some food. Volunteer at a shelter, church, or school. Visit sick children in the hospital. There are many ways you can change a person's life just by being kind.

Practice empathy. What the heck is empathy, you might ask? This basically means understanding another person's feelings, situations, and motives. So, how do you practice empathy? Are you afraid or uncomfortable around people such as gay men, lesbians, transgender, African Americans, Muslims, homeless, or folks with mental and physical disabilities? Instead of being mean to them or bullying them, take some time to volunteer and community centers where these groups congregate and strike up a conversation with them.

Get to know them. Ask questions. Listen. You just might make some new friends.

Spread joy, not rumors. Make it a goal to spread joy and sprinkle happiness everywhere you go. This world is already hard enough to navigate with illness, war, and poverty. We need no more mean people in this world.

This is not a definitive list, but this is a splendid way to get you started in your transformation from being a bully to being a champion for the people.

If you need more ideas on how to make this transformation, please visit www.BullseyeTheClown.com/transformation.

## Chapter 13
# You Are Better Than You Think You Are!

IF YOU HAVE MADE IT to this point in the book, I hope that you have picked up a nugget or two that will help you on the journey to eradicating (getting rid of) bullies from your life.

The next time a wayward bully walks your way and says an unkind word to you, you'll be ready with a few choice ways to handle the situation. If you are still at a loss, check out www.BullseyeTheClown.com/prescript for some suggestions.

Now, let's take a moment to talk about you.

Are you living up to the potential that you have set for yourself?

---

I'm not asking you if you are living up to the potential others have set for you, but are you doing what truly makes you happy?

If your answer is a resounding yes, then congratulations! You are thriving, despite what the bullies have done to you. Keep living every day doing what makes you happy.

If you answered no to that question (are you doing what truly makes you happy?), it may take a little more time to put a horse in front of your cart, so to speak.

Bullies make us stop believing in ourselves. They do not want us to be happy. For whatever reason, they get some unspeakable joy out of seeing us in turmoil. If you take a moment to reflect upon the life of the bully, they are not our role models. Bullies do not want us to live a better life than them.

I grew up with an abusive and alcoholic stepfather. He would repeatedly tell me I would never amount to anything—that I would be a loser my entire life, and I believed it, until the day I evaluated the success of my stepfather.

My stepfather was an alcoholic who spent considerable time in jail for the many DUIs that he had over the course of his life. He even had his driver's license revoked for life.

During the entire time that I have known my stepfather, he never held a permanent job. The moment he got a job, he got fired for showing up drunk. He went through several alcohol treatment programs and would joke about how he snuck beer into the hospital. To the very end he was a rebel and a rule breaker.

He was a bully telling me I would never amount to anything. He wanted to discourage me, so I would end up just like him—unemployed and unaccomplished.

Consider the source. Even if your bully is successful, and even if the world is against you...

You must always believe in yourself.

You are better than you think you are.

---

*"Do not **allow** people to dim your shine because they are **blinded**. Tell them to put on some sunglasses."*
— *Lady Gaga*

---

We are not on this earth to be miserable and unhappy. We are here on this earth to make a difference in the lives of others, and if you focus on making others happy, you will make yourself happy.

I want to empower you to apply for that job promotion, audition for that play or musical, train for that sport you want to play, ask that guy or gal out on a date.

---

*NEVER LET OTHERS BULLY OR INTIMIDATE YOU FROM LIVING YOUR BEST LIFE*

---

And while you live that best life, I want you to do good deeds and spread joy toward others. You can start by simply implementing these three things . . . (if they look familiar, it's because you just read them in the last chapter).

- **Compliment someone every day.** Find someone throughout your day that you can pay a compliment. Whether it's "Nice shirt," or "I like your shoes," an easy way to make new friends, or get others to like you, is to pay them compliments.

- **Do something nice for others.** If someone falls, help them up. Say hello to a homeless person on the street and offer to get them some food. Volunteer at a shelter, church, or school. Visit sick children in the hospital. There are many ways you can change a person's life just by being kind.

- **Spread joy.** Make it your mission to spread joy and sprinkle happiness everywhere you go. Smiles, hellos and handshakes go a long way in making this world a better place.

*FINAL THOUGHTS*
# How Clowning Cured My Bullied and Broken Soul

THERE ARE FEW PEOPLE OUT there who can't understand why I became a clown, why I continue to clown, and even how a clown is a good spokesperson for anti-bullying. So, I am going to do my best to explain that here.

My father passed away in April 2018. I had just quit a job working at a Fortune 500 company because the bullying culture in that company was so terrible. Friends promoted friends. The hardest-working employees were not only overlooked, they were told they weren't working hard enough. While some were doing twice the work, others were horsing around and even sleeping on the job.

I knew I needed to find a job after my father passed. Although I didn't quite know what exactly, I wanted to honor my father in some small way. My father was not a traveler. He might drive to the states closest to him, but in his entire life, he never stepped foot on an airplane. With some of the money my father left me, I decided to take a trip somewhere, although I wasn't sure where.

Many years prior to my father's death, I remembered watching a movie called Patch Adams, starring Robin Williams. They based the movie on a real medical doctor of the same name. After checking out his website, I discovered he did clown tours all over the world. These clown missions focused on visiting people in hospitals, orphanages, rehabilitation centers and hospices.

As luck would have it, a clown tour to Russia was happening in November 2018. I contacted Patch Adams and said I would love to do this tour, but I had zero experience as a clown. I knew I would be awful. His response was short and simple.

You are better than you think you are. Join us.

When I set out on this journey to Russia, I was harboring a lot of anger and resentment. That anger and resentment was directed toward all those bullies in my life who left me bitter, broken, and in despair. I was not living the life I wanted or dreamed. I was nothing. I had quit my job. I had no identity.

Picking up the pieces of this battered and busted life, I boarded an airplane bound for Moscow, Russia, to meet up with Patch Adams and thirty-five other clowns.

Although I did not know what I was doing (my nose was way too big and I couldn't even juggle), they gave me one simple instruction.

Your only job for the next fourteen days is to sprinkle happiness everywhere you go, and make everyone you come into contact with smile and laugh. Oh, one other thing, no whining.

It did not take long for me to witness the power and transformation clowning had on all the people we came into contact with.

For instance, at an orphanage we visited near Moscow, quite a few children besieged us. Some reached in our pockets to see what we had, some wanted to run and play, yet some sat on the outskirts of the room, not taking part.

I remember Patch's rule—to sprinkle happiness and make **everyone** laugh and smile. After spying a girl sitting all alone, I waddled my way over to her, and sat down in the chair right next to her. She looked over at me and got up and moved to a different chair away from me.

How rude, I thought.

So, I picked up my clown body, waddled back over to where she was, and sat down right next to her. She looked over at me and got up and moved again. Hmmmm . . . . I took this as a sign that she wanted to play a game.

We continued to play musical chairs until we ended up back where we started. I reached into my pocket and pulled out a small bottle of bubbles and began just blowing bubbles. The little girl was so fascinated by the bubbles that she walked right up beside me and sat down.

I looked over at her and with a smile I got up and moved to a different chair. She followed me. We ended up playing this game again until we got all the way back to where we originally started.

Both exhausted after making two trips around this large gymnasium, I handed her the bottle of bubbles and she had the best time blowing bubbles until we left. I had made a connection and made someone smile.

At another hospital, I noticed a child in a wheelchair. This child looked like he may have had cerebral palsy, but I cannot be certain. I speak English, and most of the people in Russia only speak Russian. I did not have the luxury of always asking questions and getting answers. I simply had to rely on physical jokes and gags to reach each person.

I was not really sure how to reach this child in the wheelchair. I blew up a balloon, pretended to tie it, handed it to the small boy and as he reached out to take it. I let go, and it went flying through the hall. He got the biggest kick out of that. I thought for sure after doing this once or twice he would tire of it and get bored. But no. I spent 30 minutes playing with balloons and seeing the joy on this boy's face was priceless. He lit up every time the balloon flew away.

Full disclosure: When I returned from Russia, I had no plans to clown again. It just did not seem like a viable job option, and how would I ever make money doing it? I thought, "All of those joyful faces a world away, there might be something to this whole clowning thing."

Wait a minute!

Something else happened that I didn't expect.

When I returned home, I was at peace. Where was that anger and resentment that I had before I left? It was no longer there. How did it all disappear in just fourteen short days, when I have been bottling it up for a lifetime?

What I soon realized was that while I was so focused on making others happy, I made myself happy. You can't hold two enormous emotions inside you at the same time. You can't be happy, angry. and sad all at the same time. During our tour, the happiness had to replace the anger and the sadness for the time I was in Moscow.

I would like to offer and extend that same happiness to every one of you reading this. If you practice doing nice things for other people, paying compliments everywhere you go, and sprinkling kindness in the most unlikely of places, you can experience this unspeakable joy.

- I continue to clown because I want to.

- I don't need approval.

- I don't need any authority, except my own.

- I clown because it transforms lives (my own and others).

- What better spokesperson for anti-bullying could there be?

In closing, I ask you to remember these eight things:

- Stand up for yourself and others.

- Speak out when necessary.

- Repeat these words over and over until you believe them, "I am better than I think I am."

- You are worthy of happiness and success.

- Be nice to everyone you meet.

- You can transform someone's life just by making them smile.

- Never dim your own light because others are blind.

- Be the change you want to see in the world.

# Get a Bully-Proof Blueprint

IF YOU ARE A SCHOOL, company, organization or church (yes, even churches deal with bullies), and you would like us to create a Bully-Proof Plan for you, simply log on to www.BullseyeTheClown.com/blueprint or email us a bullseye@BullseyeTheClown.com

What is a Bully-Proof Blueprint? Bully-Proof Blueprints are maps that your company or organization can use any time a bullying situation arises. It outlines who each person in your company should consult in the event they are being bullied.

This blueprint also serves as a policy and can be inserted into your company handbook. Not only should it be a road map but also a rule book. What happens when someone reports a bully? What responsibility does that person have to implement change? What should happen if someone drops the ball and doesn't do what they are supposed to do?

At no time in the life of your company or organization should you have an employee living in fear. Do your part to ensure that every one of your employees and team members has the same wonderful experience working for you. Get your Bully-Proof Blueprint today

## About the Author

**B**ORN AT A YOUNG AGE to much older parents, Bullseye The Clown (also known as Bryan Lee) has been performing for over 30 years, not always as a clown or a stand-up comedian. Bullseye even had a stint teaching drama classes for prison inmates.

He has performed at many comedy clubs, theaters and casinos across the United States. As a matter of fact, buildings have been known to collapse after Bullseye has performed there. Remember the Stardust Casino in Las Vegas?

Bullseye began his clown journey on a tour to Russia with famed clown doctor Patch Adams (made more famous by the movie starring Robin Williams). He appeared on NBC-TV's *The Caroline Rhea Show*, and in the films *Seabiscuit* and *Jason Bourne*. He currently writes for *Jest For Clowns* magazine and coaches those who have been bullied. He resides in Phoenix with his mother and dog, Lucky!

Website: http://www.BullseyeTheClown.com
Youtube: https://www.youtube.com/bullseyetheclown
Facebook (personal): http://www.facebook.com/SpeakerBryanLee
Facebook (Bullseye Page): https://www.facebook.com/bullseyetheclownonbullying/
Instagram: https://www.instagram.com/bullseye_clown/
Linkedin: https://www.linkedin.com/in/bullseyetheclown/

# GLOBAL TOUCH PRESS

Online Author workshops

A customized publication package

Personal assistance to guide you throughout the process

Editing, proof-reading, cover design, book layout and production

503.278.2677
GLOBALTOUCHPRESS.COM

I'm a writer, editor and book designer. I write fiction and nonfiction and help people on their path to publication.

503 807-4611
Jan@BearWebContent.com

Made in the USA
Middletown, DE
27 February 2022